The Little Yellow Digger

Peter Gilderdale & Fifi Colston

SCHOLASTIC
AUCKLAND SYDNEY NEW YORK LONDON TORONTO
MEXICO CITY NEW DELHI HONG KONG

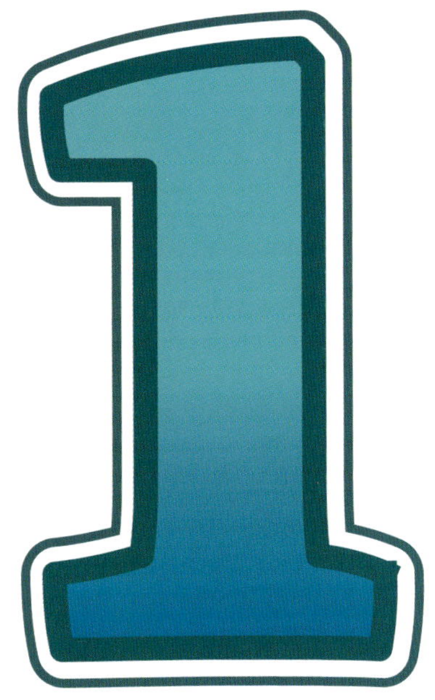

little

yellow

digger

driving up the street.

brightly coloured diggers

suddenly meet.

3

clean and shiny diggers

clattering around.

busy, working diggers

digging up the ground.

5

slightly sticky diggers

digging in a drain.

wet and dripping diggers

working in the rain.

7

splashing, sloshing diggers

driving by a flood.

8
dirty, mucky diggers
STUCK in the mud.

9

fully filthy diggers

on a muddy path.

10

diggers at the yard

have a lovely bath.

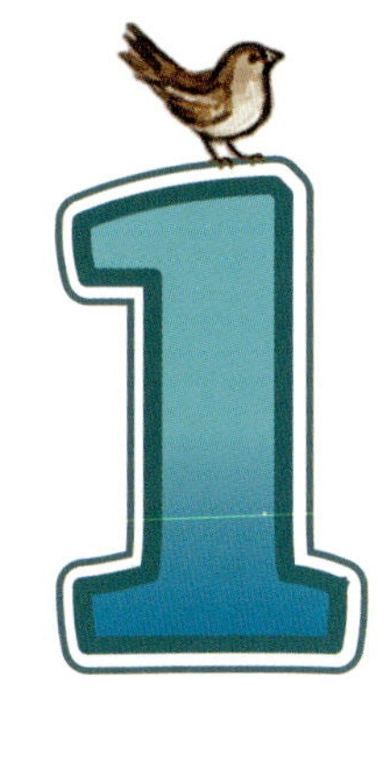

one

two

three

six

seven

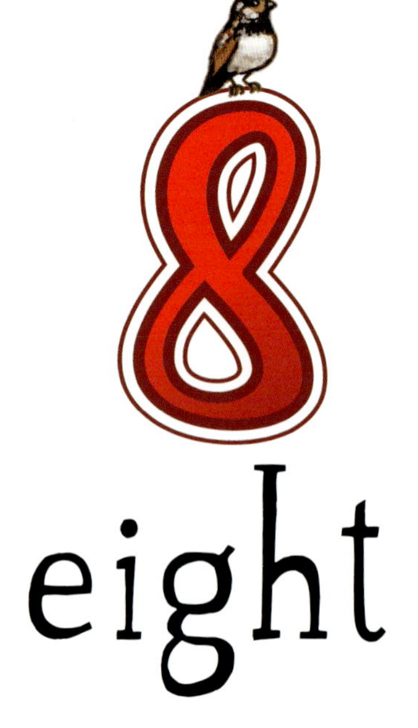

eight

four

five

nine

ten

For Orion, who (like Albie) will soon be learning how to count - P.G.

For all the teachers who persevered with teaching this arty kid maths! – F.C.

First published in 2025 by Scholastic New Zealand Limited
Private Bag 94407, Botany, Auckland 2163, New Zealand

Scholastic Australia Pty Limited
PO Box 579, Gosford, NSW 2250, Australia

ISBN 978-1-77543-956-1 (Paperback)
ISBN 978-1-77543-968-4 (Hardback)

A catalogue record for this book is available from the National Library of New Zealand.

12 11 10 9 8 7 6 5 4 3 2 1 5 6 7 8 9 / 2

Publishing team: Lynette Evans, Penny Scown and Abby Haverkamp
Designer: Smartwork Creative
Typeset in Skolar Latin
Printed in China by RR Donnelley

Scholastic New Zealand's policy is to use papers that are renewable and made efficiently from wood grown in responsibly managed forests, so as to minimise its environmental footprint.

MINI DIGGER

BACK HOE

CRAWLER

BOBCAT

FRONT-END LOADER

TRACKED EXCAVATOR

WHEELED EXCAVATOR

TWIN-CAB EXCAVATOR

OFFROAD EXCAVATOR

MINING EXCAVATOR